Cartooning

Deri Robins

MINNETONKA, MINNESOTA

This edition published in 2006 in North America by
Two-Can Publishing
11571 K-Tel Drive
Minnetonka, MN 55343
www.two-canpublishing.com

Two-Can wishes to thank artist Shannon Steven for her
help with the American terms in this book.

Library of Congress CIP data on file

ISBN 1-58728-533-9

Written by Deri Robins
Designed by Wladek Szechter/Louise Morley
Edited by Sian Morgan/Matthew Harvey
Creative Director: Louise Morley
Editorial Manager: Jean Coppendale

Credits: Corbis /Douglas Kirkland 6t
Jack Keely: 8–9, 11, 14, 18–19, 20, 25;
Roger Armstrong: 8; Don Jardine: 14;
Ed Nofziger: 17
Jim Robins 17b

Printed and bound in China

1 2 3 4 5 10 09 08 07 06

The words in **bold** are
explained in the glossary
on page 30.

Contents

Tools and materials

Anyone can draw cartoons—the more you practice, the better you'll become! This book has lots of ideas to help you improve your cartooning skills, along with projects to try out at home or at school.

Tools of the trade

All you really need is a pencil and plenty of paper. But it's good to experiment with different materials to find what works best for you. **HB** or **B** pencils are ideal for first sketches—they erase easily. Trace the final **outlines** in pen to make them last.

Cartoon experiments!

Why not try using some of the other cartooning tools? For example, markers and black ink are great for big, bold outlines. Filling in with felt-tip pens and poster paints will give your cartoons a splash of color. Colored inks and **watercolors** are good for softer hues. Remember, if you use paint or ink, draw your outlines in waterproof pen, or they will run when you start painting.

Paper

Use scrap paper for your rough ideas, and switch to smooth drawing paper for your finished cartoons.

There are lots of different materials you can use to create cartoons. As you experiment with different pens, paints, and pencils, you'll see they all create different effects.

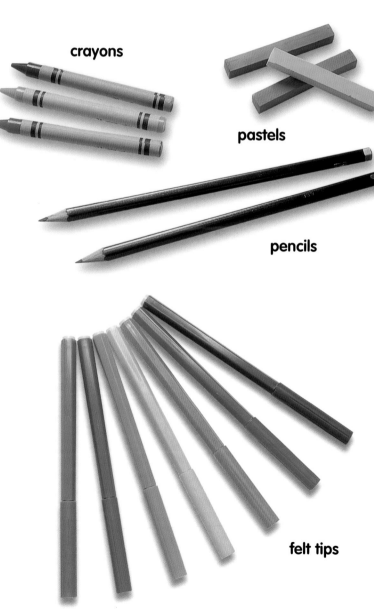

crayons

pastels

pencils

felt tips

Drawing board

You need a hard surface to support your paper when you're drawing. Use a desk or position a drawing board at a slight angle. Hold the paper in place with masking tape or thumbtacks. You need plenty of light when you are drawing, either natural sunlight or a desk lamp.

Protect your cartoons

Artwork is easily damaged. Tape your best pictures to a mount board and tape a piece of tissue paper over the top to protect it.

Keep your ideas in a notebook or sketchbook.

art paper

poster paint

colored ink

Getting started

Look for cartoon inspiration at home, at school, on vacation in the country, or during an afternoon at the beach. Start with a person, an animal, or an object that you know well, or use your imagination to create a fantasy character or monster.

What is a cartoon?

What makes cartoons different from other drawings? Think about your favorite cartoon character from movies, television, comic strips, or picture books.

The Simpsons, created by Matt Groening, are known the world over.

ANIMAL MAGIC

Look carefully at different animals and make sketches of them. Real animals might not keep still for long, so look at books, magazines, or websites on the Internet. Try to catch some wildlife shows on television or use a microscope to look at tiny insects.

People pictures

Look carefully at your family members, friends, or a favorite celebrity. Everyone has a unique **feature** that would make a great cartoon. Collect photos of people in different outfits, positions, and poses. Look at them for ideas when you draw your cartoons.

Cool cartoons

You can create different effects depending on which tools you use. Use a black pen or felt-tip marker to make outlines and add **shading.** Using felt-tips to fill in the outlines produces flat, bold color. Colored inks have a softer effect. Try different combinations to find the best one for your character.

Cartoon figures

The easiest way to draw a cartoon figure is to sketch a simple outline first, and then add the details. You can start by drawing a stick figure or by connecting rounded shapes to form a body. Try making the figure below.

Stick figures

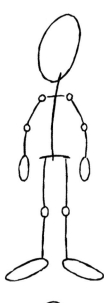

1 Draw a stick figure with ovals for its head, hands, and feet. Put small circles at the joints.

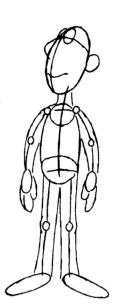

3 Draw in the basic features of the face.

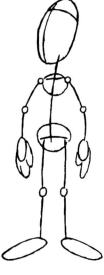

2 Build up the figure by adding more ovals for the body, such as for the shoulders and hips.

4 Finish by adding details for the face and clothing. Last of all, fill in with color.

TIP

Some people like to draw figures using circles and ovals. Stretched ovals make tall, skinny bodies, and circles make round, plump ones. Often the fun is in mixing them together!

1 Draw the outline of your figure using circles and ovals.

2 Now add details to make them funny, such as hair, shoes, and clothes.

Big and little

To draw a cartoon of somebody you know, look at them carefully. Are they tall or short? Fat or thin? Now exaggerate their most outstanding feature. Practice drawing from photographs.

Faces and features

Faces and **expressions** are important in cartoons. Start at the top. First draw the shape of the head, then add the features. Once you know what your figure looks like from the front, try a side view.

Head on

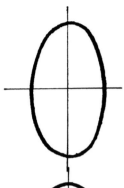

1 Draw an oval. Divide it into quarters.

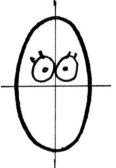

2 Put in the eyes just above the center.

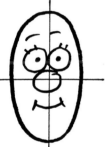

3 Add the nose on the center line. Add the mouth halfway down.

4 Add hair, eyebrows, and eyelashes. Make the face happy, sad, or scared.

TIP

Try different face shapes: long and thin, short and fat! Fat heads may have no neck. Thin heads look skinnier on a long, thin neck.

Hair can make a big difference to your characters. Different styles can make characters look messy or glamorous, young or old.

If you are making someone you know into a cartoon, look at them carefully. What do you notice most about them? Do they have a long chin? A wide face? Ears that stick out? A big nose? Glasses? These are the features you can exaggerate to make a great cartoon.

Remember glasses and jewelry. Details bring a cartoon to life!

TIP

Look at your reflection in the back of a large, shiny spoon. With your face in the light against a dark **background**, draw what you see. Your face will be stretched and distorted. Copy this for an instant cartoon effect.

Dressing up

The way you dress your cartoon characters helps to bring them to life. Uniforms and hats can tell you where their owners live, what kind of work they do, or what their personality is like.

Mix-and-match book

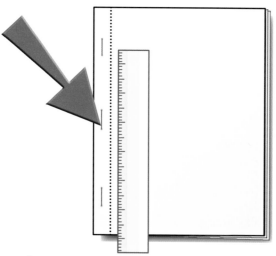

1 Staple six to eight sheets of unlined paper together to make a book. Draw a **vertical** line ¼ inch from the spine.

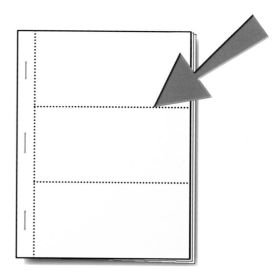

2 On the first page, use the ruler to divide the page into three equal, **horizontal** sections.

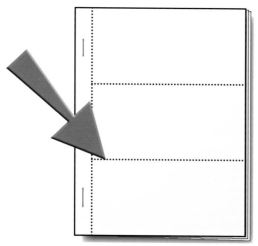

3 With an adult's help, cut along the horizontal lines from the right edge of the paper to the vertical line.

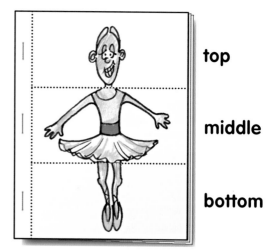

top

middle

bottom

4 Draw a cartoon character on the first page. Put the head and neck in the top third, the body in the middle, and the legs and feet in the bottom.

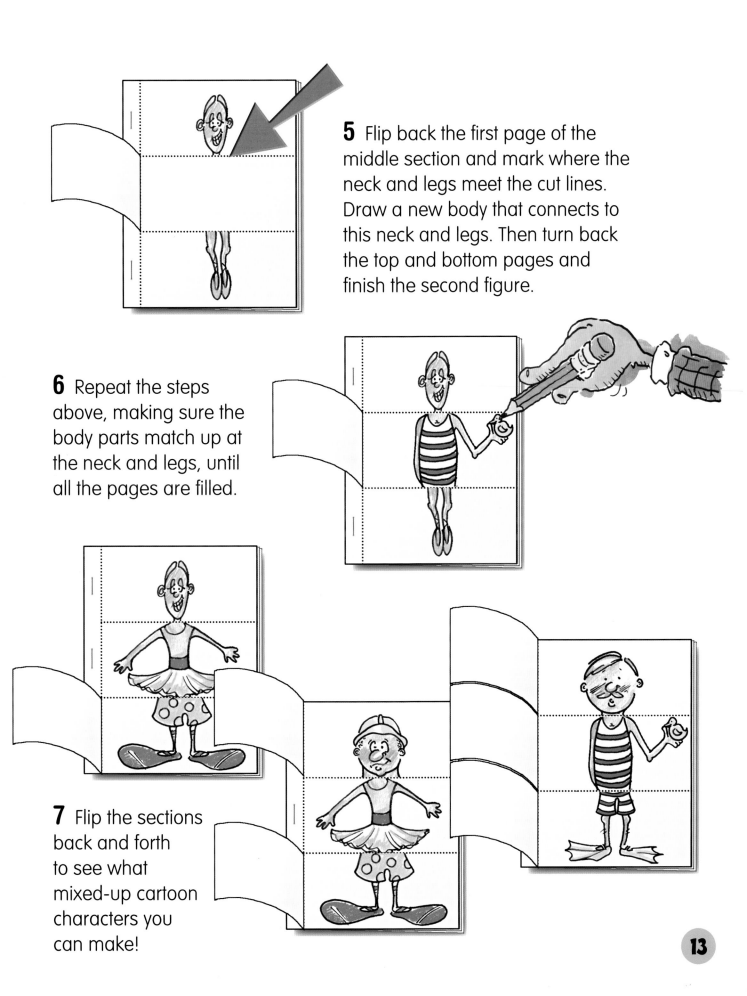

5 Flip back the first page of the middle section and mark where the neck and legs meet the cut lines. Draw a new body that connects to this neck and legs. Then turn back the top and bottom pages and finish the second figure.

6 Repeat the steps above, making sure the body parts match up at the neck and legs, until all the pages are filled.

7 Flip the sections back and forth to see what mixed-up cartoon characters you can make!

Get moving

Now that you've created your cartoon characters, you need to make them move. Before you start drawing, look at photos of people and animals on the move. Study the positions of their legs and arms.

1 Begin by drawing a simple stick figure.

2 Then add ovals and circles. Erase lines you don't want to show.

3 Now add clothes, color, and facial expressions.

Jumping

Running

Movement lines help to show which way something is moving—and how fast.

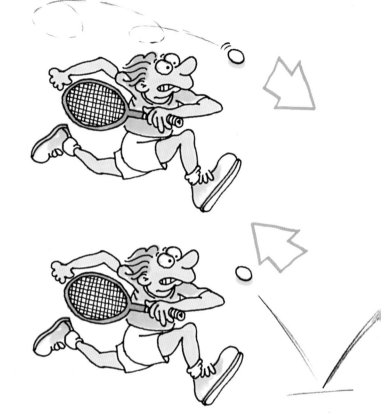

TIP

Movement lines also add extra action to your cartoon—just look at the pictures below. Adding double movement lines behind these figures makes them look more active.

Cartoon creatures

Before you start drawing cartoon animals, it's a good idea to practice sketching real ones. Then try turning your sketches into cartoons.

Drawing animals

Notice the features and personalities of a variety of animals. A dog's ears can be droopy or perky, depending on whether it is happy or sad.

KOOKY ANIMALS

You can use simple shapes to build any kind of animal.

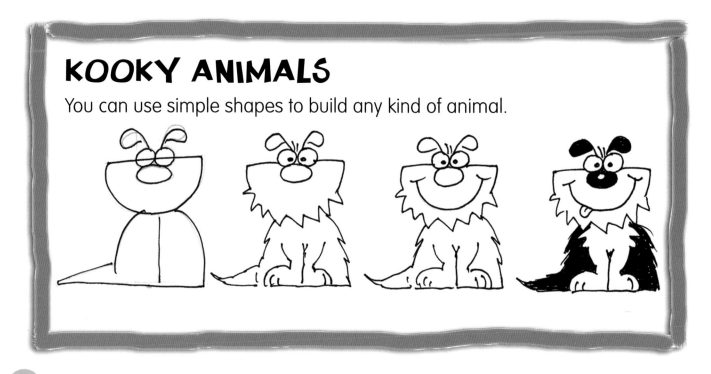

Animal shapes

1

1 Use circles and ovals to create an outline of the head and body. Add the legs, feet, and tail.

2 Erase the guide lines that you don't want in the final picture.

3 Use colored pencils or pens to finish the drawing.

2

3

When you are confident about drawing animals, try stretching the body and limbs to make them taller and skinnier, or squash them for rounder, fatter, funnier cartoon creatures.

PROJECT

Create a new animal star
Certain animals have been turned into cartoons many times before—especially bears and cats! Try to think of something more unusual and see what you can do with it. Will it be fierce or friendly? Smart or stupid? Fast or slow?

It's alive!

Cartoons can make any object come alive. Look around your kitchen, backyard, or classroom for inspiration. A house could have windows for eyes and a door for a mouth. A broom could move around by swishing its bristles.

Kitchen cartoons

Choose an object and get to know it well. Draw it so often, and from so many different angles, that it becomes as familiar as a friend.

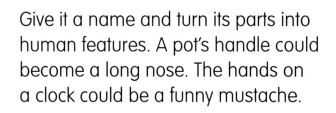

Give it a name and turn its parts into human features. A pot's handle could become a long nose. The hands on a clock could be a funny mustache.

Motor mouths

Add life to bikes, cars, scooters, skateboards, boats, trains, and buses by giving them funny faces. Try to make the shapes match the expressions. For example, a car can be round, smiley, and friendly. But make the car long and lean, with squinty headlights and a mouthful of flashing teeth, and you've got a very different character.

Monster mania

We all know that "real" monsters, such as vampires, werewolves, and ghosts, can be creepy characters. But people, animals, and even buildings can be scary too!

Everyone will recognize a vampire. How about making up your own monsters?

Wicked witches are usually ugly and have pointed noses, long chins, and warts on their faces.

1   2   3

You can draw a ghost as a black **silhouette**, or as a white, cloudy shape with a soft, black outline.

MONSTER MIX UP

Try mixing parts of different animals into a new fantasy friend--or foe!

A question of size

Even tiny creatures can become terrifying if they grow to a huge size.

PROJECT

Mythical monsters

Myths and legends are full of strange and scary creatures, such as dragons, werewolves, and devils. Choose a mythical monster and turn it into a cartoon. Will yours be scary, friendly, or funny?

Setting the scene

You've created a group of cartoon characters, but there's more to a cartoon than that. It's time to fill in the background to set the scene. Where does the cartoon take place? Is this world real, or is it a fantasy?

TIP

Always start by sketching your cartoon character in soft pencil first, and then add the background. Add **foreground** details last. When you are happy with the finished result, color it in and go over the outlines in thick, black pen.

Where to get ideas

Look at travel magazines, photos, and books, or around your house, street, or school. Which of these scenes suit your characters? Choose a few details that will tell readers where the cartoon takes place, and practice some simple backgrounds.

Placing your character

Your character should appear to be part of the scene, not just stuck on top of it. Make sure to put details in the foreground as well as the background.

Night or day?

Nighttime backgrounds are great for a spooky atmosphere. Draw your character and buildings in black silhouette.

IN THE MOOD

Different skies set the mood, too. It's easy to fill the sky with snow or rain!

Comic capers

Once you've created some amazing cartoon figures, you can use them to lay out a comic story. First, take a look at some of your favorite comics. Some are laid out in a row, and others fill a page or even a whole book. What format will fit your characters and the setting best?

Frames

A comic strip is divided into sections called **frames.** They may be squares, circles, ovals, or a combination. Experiment with jagged or bumpy shapes, or let some parts of the picture break out of the frame edges. You can use a ruler, or draw the frames by hand.

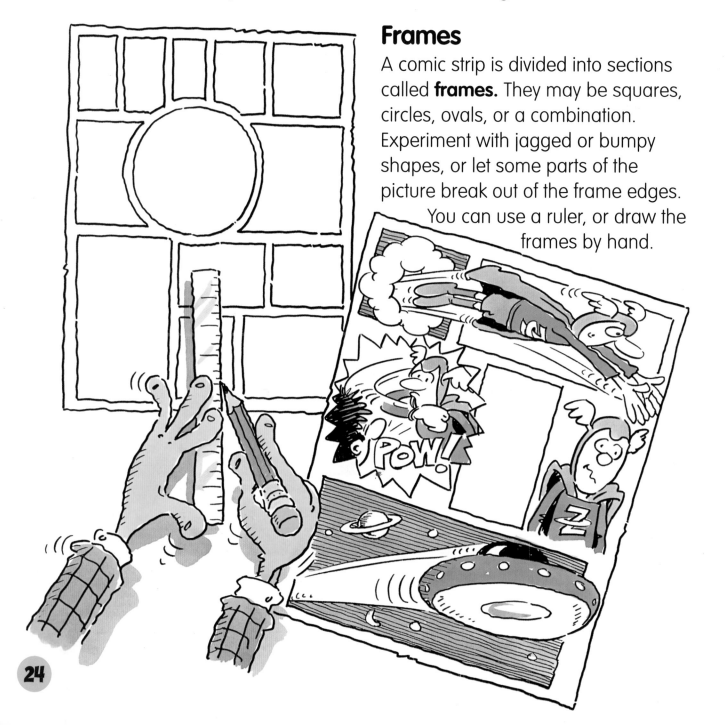

Storylines

In comic strips, the story is often told through characters' words and thoughts. Speech bubbles are usually oval, with a tail that stretches to the speaker's mouth. Thought bubbles are connected to the thinker by a string of smaller bubbles. If you want to include extra information, and you have enough space, make a box at the top or bottom of the picture to write in.

Exclamation marks!

These punctuation marks are used a lot in comics! To show people shouting, use a thick black marker.

TIP

Speech and thought bubbles usually go in the top third of the picture, so draw your sketch in the bottom two-thirds.

Making a comic strip

YOUR CARTOON CHARACTER CAN DO ANYTHING!

Now that you know the basics, try creating a comic strip with your own cast of funny, scary, or silly characters.

Lights, camera, action!

Making a comic strip is like making a movie: you need a story, a main character, a few minor characters, and a series of backgrounds. Start by thinking up a short, simple story with a beginning, a middle, and an end. Look through some joke books for ideas for a funny ending.

Stars of the show

What will your main character look like? Decide what sort of personality they have and think of a name. Try drawing them from lots of different angles to get them right. You also need friends and enemies for the main character to talk to. Try not to use more than three characters, or readers may get confused.

Storyboarding

You're ready to make a **storyboard**. This is a rough sketch of each frame; it doesn't have to be perfect. Try to vary the pictures. Sometimes characters can be in the distance, other times you can show a close-up of their face.

Comic frames

When your storyboard is finished, it's time to turn it into a finished comic strip. Draw each frame as neatly as you can. Use pencil, and make sure each frame is big enough for what you want to include.

Filling in the details

Now it's time to copy your drawings from the storyboard. Switch to drawing paper if you've been using scrap paper so your finished cartoons look their best. First, draw in the outlines in pencil.

Go over the outlines with black marker or felt-tip. When the outlines are dry, color them in. Your comic strip is complete!

Making movies

In an **animated** cartoon, thousands of pictures are shown at the rate of twenty-four pictures per second. This is too fast for our eyes to see, so it looks to us as if the objects in the pictures are moving. These twelve pictures would fill just half a second in an animated cartoon:

Make a flip book

Make a simple flip book to see your cartoons really move! You will need a small, unlined notebook and a pen or pencil. Decide what action you want to see animated—a person kicking a ball for example. Then think about what your arms and legs do when you kick a ball.

1 On a scrap of paper, from left to right, sketch about twenty stick figures. Change the position of the arms and legs slightly each time so that the figure gradually performs the action.

2 Copy the first figure to the bottom corner of the first page of the book.

3 Draw the second figure in the same place on the bottom corner of the next page. Keep going until you have drawn all the figures.

4 Bend the book slightly, with your thumb at the edge of the pages, and flip through the pages. Your figure will appear to move! This is similar to how animated movies are made.

Practice drawing different types of movements. Ask a friend to perform the movements for you to copy, or look at your reflection in a mirror.

TIP

Animators use **key drawings** to work out a series of movements. If you want to draw someone running, jumping, or just drinking a cup of coffee, draw the start, middle, and end positions. These are your key drawings. Now you can draw the positions in between to complete the series.

Glossary

animated   appearing to be moving. Animated cartoons are pictures that seem to move because they flash by quickly.

B   a soft type of pencil. Even softer ones are marked 2B, 3B, etc., up to 6B.

background   the area in the back of a picture, behind the main object

expression   the look on a person's face.

feature   the ears, nose, eyes, or other part of the face. Differences in our features is what makes us all look different

foreground   the area at the front of a picture, between the viewer and the main object of the picture

frames   the boxes that make up a comic strip or a page of a comic book

HB   a medium-hard type of pencil. Harder pencils are marked 2H, 3H, etc., to 6H.

horizontal   from side to side

key drawings   drawings that show the beginning and ending positions in an action or movement, and at least one position in the middle. These drawings are used to map out how the action will go before drawing all of the positions in between.

outlines   the lines that form the outer edge of something

shading   darker areas of color added to a picture

silhouette   a drawing of an object that is filled in with a dark color so that you only see its shape, not details such as color or texture

storyboard   a series of rough drawings in which a cartoonist figures out how the story will unfold and what each frame will show

vertical   up and down

watercolors   dry paints that are mixed with water before they are used

Index

Notes for parents and teachers

The cartoon projects in this book can be used as stand-alone projects or as a part of other areas of study. While the ideas in the book are offered as inspiration, children should always be encouraged to draw from their imagination and first-hand observation.

Sourcing ideas
Whenever possible, art projects should tap into children's interests and be relevant to their lives and experiences. Try using stimulating starting points, such as friends, family, or pets, vacations, hobbies, television shows, or current affairs.

Encourage children to source their own ideas and references from comics, books, magazines, or the Internet.

Digital cameras are handy for recording reference materials (landscapes, people, or animals) that can be printed out to look at while drawing.

Other lessons can be an ideal springboard for a cartooning project—a school trip or a story from Greek mythology could be retold in cartoon-strip form. Get the children to look at the way that picture-book illustrators have used cartoon strips to retell history, legends, and stories from literature.

Encourage children to keep a sketchbook to draw their ideas, and to collect images and objects to help them develop their cartoons.

If you have access to a video camera, have children storyboard a simple animated cartoon sequence and shoot it frame by frame to see how well it works. Encourage the children to think of music and sound effects to go with their cartoon. They could even make the instruments they need from everyday objects.

Characters for animated cartoons can also be created from other media, such as clay or Plasticine. Move the models a little at a time and record each position, then use video editing software to string them together.

Evaluating work
It's important and motivating for children to share their work with others, and to compare ideas and methods. Encourage them to talk about their work. What do they like best about it? How would they do it differently next time?

Show the children examples of other artists' work. How did they tackle the same subject and problems? Do the children like the work? Why or why not?

Help children to recognize the originality and value of their work, to appreciate the different qualities in others' work, and to respect ways of working that are different from their own. Display children's work for all to admire!

Going further
Look at ways to develop extensions to a project. For example, adapt cartoons to make printed T-shirts, cards, pins, or characters for board games. Use image-enhancing computer software and digital scanners to enhance, build up, and juxtapose images in interesting and funny ways.

Help your artist(s) set up an art gallery to show off their work, or scan artwork and post the images to a photo website where others can log in and view them. Having their work displayed professionally will make them feel that their work is valued.